Digging for SUE

by Susan Evento

Chapter 1
The Mighty T. Rex

Tyrannosaurus rex were huge, fierce animals. They walked on two legs. They ruled Earth millions of years ago. How do we know this?

T. rex bones were first found around 1900. Then parts of more T. rex **skeletons** were found. Scientific research was done on these **fossils**. In 1990, an exciting new discovery took place.

Tyrannosaurus rex means "king of the tyrant lizards."

Sue made her discovery right before she was about to leave.

In 1990, Sue Hendrickson was part of an exploration for fossils in South Dakota. One day, Sue and her dog, Gypsy, walked to some nearby cliffs. Her group had not yet searched there.

Sue noticed a few small bones on the ground. Then she spotted some huge bones sticking out of the cliff. Sue saw that the bones were hollow. This meant that they came from a meat-eating dinosaur. Sue knew T. rex had lived in this part of North America. She was excited by her important discovery!

Chapter 2
The Dig

Sue and other fossil hunters started to dig into these cliffs. They didn't use machines. That could cause damage to the bones. Instead, they used picks and shovels. After five days of teamwork, they reached the bones 30 feet down.

Fossil hunters may spend hours searching for tiny pieces of bone.

Sue's enormous jaw holds very sharp teeth up to 12 inches long.

Then they had to work more carefully. They used smaller tools. They kept finding bones. Some were huge. The skull was about five feet long! Finally, the hunters found almost all of the dinosaur's bones. They were in excellent shape. The hunters named this T. rex *Sue*. They named her after the woman who found her. But scientists still do not know if Sue was male or female.

The diggers took photographs as they dug. They numbered the bones. They wrote notes about them. Later, they would be able to put the bones together to form the skeleton. Many bones were in the same position they were in millions of years ago. Some were mixed up. A few were missing.

Diggers need to work carefully to uncover bones.

The diggers left some rock around the bones. This would help protect them. Then the diggers covered the fossils with layers of cloth. The cloth was soaked in plaster. As the plaster dried, it would harden. It would protect the bones the same way a cast protects a person's broken bone.

For a few years, people fought over who had the right to Sue's bones. Finally, Sue's bones found their home. She was brought to the Field Museum in Chicago.

Diggers label the plaster to help them remember what they found where.

Chapter 3
At the Museum

Sue's skull took more than 3,500 hours to clean.

People at the museum had to do a lot of work to prepare the bones. More than 250 bones needed to be cleaned and studied. First, workers had to remove the plaster. Then, they had to remove the rock around the bones. They used special tools, such as tiny jack hammers. As they got closer to the bone, they used even smaller tools.

This team used a **CT scanner** to take **X-rays** of the inside of the bones. Sue's enormous skull wouldn't fit into the scanner. So the team shipped it to a place where they scan airplane parts for problems. Sue's skull just fit!

This is the X-ray scan of Sue's skull.

Putting a dinosaur skeleton together is hard. Sue's team fixed cracks in the bones. They used a special glue. They also used a material like modeling clay to repair missing bone parts. Sue was missing an arm, a foot, and a few back bones. Workers used the bones they had to make models of the missing ones.

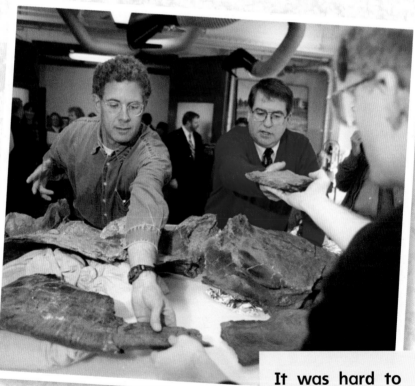

It was hard to fit the bones together.

They also made casts of each bone. This way, exact copies of the entire skeleton could be displayed elsewhere. Next, the workers had another huge job. They had to put all the pieces together.

It can take thousands of hours to get a skeleton ready for display.

They needed a special frame to hold the bones up. But Sue's skull was too heavy to be placed on top. So they made a lighter plastic cast of the skull. They placed the real skull in a special case.

Sue's skull is too big and heavy to lift easily.

We still don't know why T. rex had such small arms. But we know they were strong. Scientists can tell this because the huge arm muscles left marks on Sue's bones. The scans also show that Sue had a great sense of smell. They show that some T. rex bones were in the same position as bird bones. This and other features might mean that today's birds are relatives of T. rex.

What have we learned about Sue? She was about 41 feet long. She stood about 12 feet high from the hip. She weighed about 9 tons. And she died at about age 28.

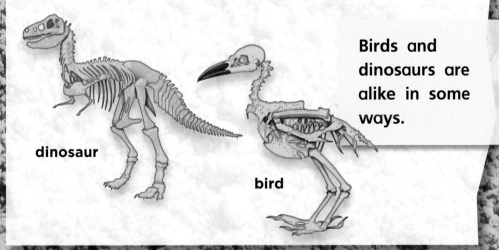

dinosaur

bird

Birds and dinosaurs are alike in some ways.

Sue is the first thing visitors see at the Field Museum.

Nearly 10 years after her discovery, Sue was displayed in the Field Museum. Millions of people have visited Sue.

Sue is the largest T. rex ever found. Her fossils are the most complete. They are also in the best condition.

As a result of Sue's discovery, we know more about dinosaurs. New fossils help us understand the past. They show how animals have changed over time.

Respond to Reading

Summarize

Use details to help you summarize *Digging for Sue.*

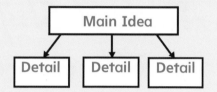

Text Evidence

1. How do you know *Digging for Sue* is expository text? Genre

2. What is the main idea on page 8? What are the key details that support it? Main Idea and Key Details

3. Use what you know about Greek roots to figure out the meaning of *dinosaur* on page 3. Greek and Latin Roots

4. Write about what fossil hunters do to prepare bones. Write About Reading

Compare Texts
Read about how teams explore.

Ancient Ship Discovered!

In 2010, a machine was digging at the site of the new World Trade Center in New York City. Suddenly, it hit something hard. It was the wooden body of an ancient ship!

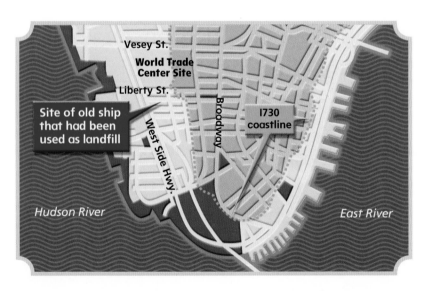

Vesey St.

World Trade
Center Site

Liberty St.

Site of old ship that had been used as landfill

West Side Hwy.

Broadway

1730 coastline

Hudson River

East River

Workers found the ship 20 feet underground.

Illustration: Bob Schuster

Scientists measured and labeled what they found at the site.

Scientists hurried to the site. They needed to dig up the ship quickly. The air would soon destroy the wood. Many people carried parts of the ship by hand from the site by hand.

Scientists found a coin and a shoe buckle.

Scientists studied the rings in this ship's wood to find out when it was built. They think it was built between 1770 and 1780. It probably carried goods to sell. Perhaps it sailed on the Hudson River.

Scientists hope that more secrets of the ship will be discovered!

Mark Lennihan/AP Images

Make Connections

How do scientists use teamwork?
Essential Question

How did the scientists in both selections protect the items they found? Text to Text

Glossary

CT scanner *(SEE TEE SKAN-ur)* machine that takes X-rays and lets doctors look inside bodies *(page 9)*

fossils *(FOS-uhlz)* hardened remains of animals or plants that lived long ago *(page 2)*

skeletons *(SKEL-uh-tuhnz)* frames that support and protect the bodies of animals *(page 2)*

X-rays *(EKS-rayz)* pictures taken of the inside of bodies *(page 9)*

Index

Focus on
Science

Purpose To find out how teamwork helps you explore

What to Do

Step 1 ▶ Think about a time when you worked with others to explore a place or thing.

Step 2 ▶ Create a chart like this one.

Team Members	What We Did

Conclusion Share your chart with the class. Talk about how working as a team made your job easier. Tell them what your team learned about the thing or place you explored.